# This Is Crazy!

## A Mother's Heart

CYNTHIA WILLIAMS

WESTBOW·
PRESS
A DIVISION OF THOMAS NELSON
& ZONDERVAN

Scripture taken from the Holy Bible, NEW INTERNATIONAL VERSION®.
Copyright © 1973, 1978, 1984 by Biblica, Inc. All rights reserved worldwide.
Used by permission. NEW INTERNATIONAL VERSION® and NIV® are
registered trademarks of Biblica, Inc. Use of either trademark for the offering of
goods or services requires the prior written consent of Biblica US, Inc.

Scripture taken from the New King James Version. Copyright © 1979, 1980,
1982 by Thomas Nelson, Inc. Used by permission. All rights reserved.

Scripture taken from the Amplified Bible, copyright © 1954, 1958, 1962,
1964, 1965, 1987 by The Lockman Foundation. Used by permission.

WestBow Press books may be ordered through booksellers or by contacting:

WestBow Press
A Division of Thomas Nelson & Zondervan
1663 Liberty Drive
Bloomington, IN 47403
www.westbowpress.com
1 (866) 928-1240

Because of the dynamic nature of the Internet, any web addresses or links contained in
this book may have changed since publication and may no longer be valid. The views
expressed in this work are solely those of the author and do not necessarily reflect the
views of the publisher, and the publisher hereby disclaims any responsibility for them.

Any people depicted in stock imagery provided by Thinkstock are models,
and such images are being used for illustrative purposes only.
Certain stock imagery © Thinkstock.

ISBN: 978-1-4908-7171-4 (sc)
ISBN: 978-1-4908-7172-1 (e)

Library of Congress Control Number: 2015903291

Print information available on the last page.

WestBow Press rev. date: 4/2/2015

# Dedication & Acknowledgments

To My Lord and Savior Jesus Christ

What a privilege to dedicate this book in memory of my loving son DeMarco "Cocoa" McCarter. To my husband, Darryl, and daughter Valencia thank you for your love and support. To my parents Lee Arthur McCarter Sr., and Fannie Davis Caldwell, thank you for always being there for me.

To my sister Lisa Tarrant, Cousin Barbara Mims, and friend Tayloria Green thank you for your listening ear. To my family and friends thank you for all your love and encouragement. To my mother in-law Mary N. Williams, thanks for being my class support partner. Thanks to Pastor Michael & Tayloria Green and The Embassy Church family for your encouragement and prayers, and all others who encouraged me in this journey.

A special thanks to Wilhemenia Hogg, Lisa Tarrant, and Stephanie Thompson, for the sacrifice and contribution that you made in the efforts in editing this book. Thank you Randy Tarrant for working the book. This would not be possible without each of you.

# Contents

# *Foreword*

osing a loved one or something you care deeply about is a very painful and traumatic experience. Many people associate this pain with all kinds of emotions and often times may feel like the sadness or pain will never go away. These reactions are normal when dealing with significant loss. However, while there is no wrong or right way to grieve, there are healthy ways to cope with the pain. This book is an excellent example of how one can do so in a healthly way. As stated in the book "This is Crazy" Author and renowned writer, Cynthia McCarter Williams describes grief as a natural response to loss. In fact grief is an emotional suffering that one may feel when something or someone you love has been taken away.

Grieving is a highly individual and personal experience. How one grieves depends on various factors, including personality and coping styles, life experience, the nature of the loss and most importantly ones faith. The grieving process takes time. As healing happens gradually; the author's excerpts further displays this concept throughout the book; in fact there is no **"normal" timetable for grieving.** Whatever your grief experience is, it is important to be patient with yourself and allow the process to naturally unfold. Cynthia's book provides a framework for the healing process her exercises and journal opportunities further support one as they may experience the "five stages of grief" as illustrated by psychiatrist Elisabeth Kübler-Ross.

**The five stages of grief:**

- **Denial:** "This can't be happening to me."
- **Anger:** "*Why* is this happening? Who is to blame?"
- **Bargaining:** "Make this not happen, and in return I will _____."
- **Depression:** "I'm too sad to do anything."
- **Acceptance:** "I'm at peace with what happened."

If you are experiencing any of these emotions following a loss, it may help to know that your reaction is natural and that you'll heal in time. Contrary to popular belief, **you do not have to go through each stage in order to heal.** In fact, the responses to any loss are typical. The book "This is Crazy" will offer those reading an opportunity to laugh, cry, relate, learn and more importantly heal in a healthy way while getting a dose of spiritual cleansing. I am honored to have been given the opportunity to write this Foreword as a professional whom has worked as a therapist in the field of Mental Health I am delighted and evermore grateful to be a part of such great works. The stigma associated with Mental Health is real furthermore the sooner you acknowledge the sooner the healing can begin.

Jennifer Cobbs, LMSW

# Preface

Grief is a part of life for everyone, but how does one grieve after a loss? Any one, at any given time can experience grief and loss; it can be sudden or expected. Often times when an individual experience grief from a loss (death, divorce, loss of job, loss of pet, etc.), they may choose different ways to express it. We are all different, and will respond differently even in the event of experiencing the same loss.

The question is, how do I handle grief and can I mourn in a healthy way? The answer is to embrace it! Yes, you can mourn in a healthy way; however, oftentimes people are grieving alone for various reasons. Some may feel that they can handle it by themselves. Some may not want others to know how they truly feel, especially if they are a Christian. Ironically, those who are not Christian tends to do the same. So often, we hear people say… "Everything is going to be okay, or just continue with life or stay busy when you go back to work. Things will get better. Hold your head up, God has you, just remember the story of Job in the bible and all he went through."

Many individuals look for their pastor and church members to help them feel better during their time of grief. Oftentimes, support is provided only during the first stage of loss, unless the church provides an on-going grief support ministry. It is important that any church grief program encourages individuals to seek professional help if needed. If a qualified or well trained professional is not in place, the support may be inadequate. We so often provide them with scriptures and a prayer and tell them in time they will be okay. The information given is necessary the prayers and scriptures are beneficial; however this does not always register with a person at that time.

Reluctance to seek professional help seems to be more prevalent in low social economical communities. I believe it is due to the lack of knowledge and/or not wanting to be embarrassed about seeking help for fear of what others may say or think. Particularly, when it comes from family members who don't quite seem to understand what you are going through (your grief). It is important to understand that you can grieve in a healthy way, without feeling ashamed or even embarrassed; especially, when additional support is necessary for your healing. It must be understood that God is our ultimate healer and it is the responsibility of each individual to seek the necessary help needed to cope and grieve healthy.

The word of God tell us in Luke 4:18 (NKJV) that "The Spirit of the Lord is upon Me,

Because He has anointed Me to preach the gospel to the poor; He has sent Me to heal the brokenhearted, To proclaim liberty to the captives And recovery of sight to the blind,

To set at liberty those who are oppressed." God will heal your broken heart!


This book is written from a personal experience to educate, encourage, and to inform others that you can grieve in a healthy way. This book is not meant to take the place of a licensed professional grief counselor or support group; however, it's a tool to help you go through the grieving process in a healthy way. It will allow you to be honest about how you truly feel without feeling misunderstood. My prayer is at the end of this book, whether read alone, in a group setting, book club or even in the marketplace as a tool for employers. Individual will be empowered to face their life challenges. Let's take a look at the stages of grief: denial, anger, blaming, depression and acceptance.

Blessings,
Cynthia McCarter Williams

# Introduction

G rief will hit our homes in one way or another. The question is when it hits, how will you handle it? Well, little did I know, I would have to experience grief in a way that I never had before. On August 2, 2007 around 2:45 a.m., I received a phone called from my son's job informing me that he was killed in a trucking accident. I screamed from the depth of my soul while slowly going to the floor in disbelief. In an unexpected instance, I was in a whirlwind. I just kept saying this is unbelievable… This is Crazy! Little did I know that I would be saying, this phrase over and over again for many reasons and for many years.

I was in a total state of shock. I immediately begin to say God help me my emotions were high. Boy! What bad timing to have something like this happen. You see it was two days before our major Women Empowering Women for the Next Generation, Inc. (WEW), women and girls' conference and retreat. I told my dear friend Tayloria that I needed her help because the conference will go on. My husband, Darryl asked me was I sure about that decision? I told him right now this was the best thing for me. In all things, God will get the Glory even in death.

The WEW, team stepped up to the plate, kept their focus and did what God had instructed us to do. Ministry, even in the mist of pain! I was still saying this is unbelievable… This is crazy! Many people were in disbelief and others were wondering "how could she do this when her son just died." I shared with them that God has me covered and that I was secure in my spirit, but as a mother I hurt.

As different people came to my home, to show support, I heard the many clichés… "Sorry for your loss", "God doesn't make mistakes", "time will heal the pain", and "I know what you are going through." I heard them…but I didn't… I was numb and in total shock. I would cry, but as more people began to show up, I dried up my tears. In my head, I was saying… God… they really don't know how I feel…because, I do not know how I feel (I knew that they meant well). I said, "Lord, help me to get pass this weekend" and he did. Oh, yes God was glorified at the retreat and many were blessed. We had an awesome celebration of my son's home-going, but I was still in shock.

I begin to say to family and friends; I'm going to get myself some help. They didn't really know what to say, but the look on their faces said it all. I was glad my mother-in-law Mary, was not embarrassed to share that she went to a grief support group, after the death of her husband the previous year. She shared how it really helped her, because everyone was there for the same reason. They were all trying to deal with grief.

In the beginning I had a lot of support and lots of phone calls, cards, you name it. People did what they knew to do. I was shown a lot of love, but I was still in shock. I kept hearing in time it will get better. God will give you strength, so on and so on. I just wanted to scream, because I knew all of that. I just wanted to tell them… Saying all of that doesn't stop the pain. All I wanted to know is, how do I deal with this? Instead of saying what was on my mind, I would simply say… "Just say pray for me".

I told my husband that I wanted to grieve and mourn in a healthy way, without spiritualizing everything. How do I deal with the natural man without feeling crazy? I kept saying "this is crazy I need real help." Real help, is just what I will get to maintain my sanity.

This was my prayer,

Lord, here I am… I am wondering aimlessly, I do not know what life holds for me. I know there is a new life. I don't know what directions to go in. Lord, today I am trying to understand and deal with grief, and deal with the death of my son. Help me Lord! Teach me your ways. I know you love me God. I know that I am the apple of your eye. Help me to understand this process that I am going through. This is a process that everyone must go through, I know it seems like a great storm in my life and it truly is. I know that I am going to be okay, because you are truly an awesome God.

I have many questions and I am seeking answers. I know others will share their grief, but this is my grief. This is my grief! My personal grief that I must go through. I must face it head on and without fear. I have to believe and trust you. I have to stand on your word, and believe your promises that you will shield me. You will protect me and give me peace in the midst of this storm. So today, God I thank you. I bless your Holy name as you continue to lead and direct me. Help me so I can help others. In Jesus' name.

Amen

# Chapter 1

# What Now?

*I* was desperately seeking help in my shattered world of grief and loss. What is grief? Is there a difference between grief and mourning? I knew my search for understanding was the key to my healing. My process began when I went to a grief support group. The first day of my support class was very interesting. I was a new face in the group. The very first thing that I had to do was to state my name and tell why I was there... Reality check! I was given a handout, and I begin to look at the bottom of the page. It said, "American Cancer Society Life After Loss Bereavement Support Group."

My eyes went back to the top of the page, and I saw "grief" defined as a life shaking sorrow over a loss. It can be painful, frightening, and overwhelming. Many people experiencing grief doubt that their feelings and responses are right; even doubt that their behavior is okay. I looked at the meaning, but it did not settle me. We were given a sheet with indicators on it, and the indicators were a list of emotions that fell under these categories: Physical/Behavioral, Emotional/ Social, and Intellectual.

I started listening to the group as they expressed their feelings. One lady said she could not cry. I was thinking to myself that is where I am now, crying on the inside. I could not shed any tears. The counselor turns to me and asks if I would like to share my feelings. I said sure, and I begin to say I do not believe this I am numb! I have no feelings, and I am in a state of shock! She in turns said that is normal. My eyes watered, and I said to myself normal… Wow! I thought something was wrong with me.

I went home and shared the information with my husband (he could not make the class because of work). My prayer for that night was Lord, let me get past the shock so that I can deal with reality. I want to grief healthy. My understanding of grief and mourning became clear. Grief is all of my feelings (indicators) and thoughts on the inside from the result of my loss. While mourning is expressing what's on the inside outwardly. We'll at least this is how I understand it!

In life, we go through different stages, and there are different stages in dealing with grief and loss. The day came when I had to deal with reality. In my second week of class and with others I finally admitted that I would never see my son again. I said this over and over again until the reality was real. Wow, it seemed as though my pain got worse. My head was hurting as if someone hit me over the head with a hammer. I did not say a lot that day. I just kept circling my indicators.

**Note:** Bereavement for all of us is a normal part of life; however, dealing with grief, with limited or no support is not only unhealthy for the mind, body and soul, but could be downright dangerous for the spirit.

People may experience the same type of loss and have completely different reactions on how they deal with their loss during the grieving process. A loss may come in many forms: the loss of a relationship (love one, friend, or pet), loss of a home, job, and etc. While some losses may appear more serious than others, the stages of the grief process are the same. Make a decision to understand the stages of grief and allow yourself the opportunity to grieve.

**Matthew 7:7 (NIV)**
"Ask and it will be given to you: ***seek*** and you will find: knock and the door will be opened to you.

The question and response section is to help you express how you feel. I encourage you to be honest with your answers. Whether you choose to share your answers with others or not. Remember everyone grieves and mourns differently. There is no time limit. Journaling is encouraged to help you release, remember and heal.

### *God will heal your broken heart!*

**Psalm 22:8 (NIV)**
*"He trusts in the Lord: let the LORD rescue him. Let him deliver him, since he delights in him."*

1. In your own words, what is your understanding of grief and mourning?

    _____

    _____

    _____

    _____

    _____

    _____

    _____

    _____

2. What is loss?

    _____

    _____

    _____

    _____

    _____

    _____

    _____

    _____

3. What state are you in shock or reality? If your answer is **shock** take time to **acknowledge** the **reality** of the loss. How do you feel?

_____

_____

_____

_____

_____

_____

_____

4. Replaying the reality is normal, how many times have you replayed the events surrounding the loss? How do you feel (Be patient, it is a process)?

_____

_____

_____

_____

_____

_____

_____

5. What are some of your indicators (See the next pages for the list of indicators)?

_____

_____

_____

_____

_____

_____

_____

# GRIEF INDICATORS

Physical/Behavioral, Emotional/Social and Intellectual Responses to Loss.

## Physical or Behavioral

Accident proneness
Alcohol or drug abuse
Allergies
Arthritis
Asthma
Backaches
Breathing deeply
Breathing difficulty
Breathing shallow
Chest tightness
High Cholesterol
Constipation
Cramps
Diarrhea
Dizziness
Dry mouth
Eye pain
Eye squinting
Face downcast
Face flushed
Fainting spells
Forehead raised, wrinkled
Frowning
Gait slowed
Shortness of breath
Sleeping to much
Shoulders raised

Sighing
Slumped posture
Nightmares
Numb or tingling extremities
Overeating
Sneezing
Speech slowed
Stomach ace
Stomach butterflies
Stomach gas
Stomach ulcer
Sweating

## Emotional or Social

Agitation
Anger
Angry outburst
Anxious, general/specific
Blaming others
Critical of oneself
Crying
Depression
Difficulty in relationships
Dread
Grinding teeth
Hands cold
Hay Fever
Heart rate increased

High blood pressure
Hives, rash, itching
Incoordination
Insomnia
Loss of appetite
Low resistance & minor illness
Migraine headaches
Muscle tightness in face
Teeth clenching
Tightness back of neck, shoulders, back, stomach, thighs, calves, and feet
Nausea (recurrent)
Fear of groups or crowds
Guilt feelings
Indecisive
Irritability
Jealousy
Lack of initiative
Loss of interest in living
Moodiness
Restlessness
Sadness
Suspiciousness

## Intellectual

Concentration difficulty
Errors in judging distance
Errors in language (grammar, enunciation, pronunciation)
Errors in numbers
Fantasy life lessened
Forgetfulness
Inattention
Lack of attention to details
Lack of awareness to external events
Loss of creativity
Loss of productivity
Memory loss
Mental blocking
Overly attentive to details
Past oriented rather present or future
Preoccupation
Rumination
Thoughts of death or suicide or worrying

# Journal

*Cynthia Williams*

# Chapter 2

# Trying to Cope

It seemed like a long week before my next class. My emotions were high, and I was going through the stages of grief. I finally got past the shock, and then I started blaming myself. I was saying, what if I would have or maybe I could have done… I begin to say Lord; I need answers, and I do not understand. I would burst out crying. I couldn't function, and I could not think. Boy, I was indecisive and restless. My eyes were hurting from crying and the lack of sleep.

My husband was experiencing some of the same things. He told me it was an accident, and there was nothing we could have done or said to prevent it. He said Cent; it was just a motor vehicle accident. I said in anger, WHY MY SON HAD TO DIE and WHY DID THE OTHER GUY LIVE (you see…there was another driver in the truck with my son, in the back of the cab sleeping….waiting on his turn to drive)? Darryl, my husband, said, "Cent I do not know." You know the word of God better than I do. Are you questioning God? I stopped for an instance, in all of my pain and said only God knows.

I was trying to deal with the reality of it all. I begin to cope by focusing on how happy my son was. Friends would come by to get me out of the house. I started projects that I did not complete. I was trying everything to get some normalcy, but it did not work. It was a process that I had to go through. The one thing I did realize was that I needed help from God. He was the only one that could help me through this,

9

because I was a total wreck. Every day I would say God keep me in my right mind. I would listen to spiritual songs and watch Christian television stations. I did this even if I did not feel like it or even if I was not paying attention to it.

It was necessary for my spirit and soul. In our next class session, the counselor asked how our week was. I told her that I had a hard week. As other members of the group begin to share, the counselor said something that changed my life! She told us that we must embrace the loss, and we need to confront it head on. She told us to take time out every day to mourn. Reflect on the memories, and even look at pictures if we could. I said to myself, I am going to do everything she said. I do not want to be in denial, and I do not wish to be stuck in this stage. I just want to understand.

1. List those things that helped you cope this week.

   _____
   _____
   _____
   _____
   _____
   _____
   _____
   _____

2. Were they healthy or unhealthy?

   _____
   _____
   _____
   _____
   _____
   _____
   _____
   _____

3. What are some of the unhealthy things you did to help you cope with loss? Did it make the situation better or worse?

_____
_____
_____
_____
_____
_____
_____
_____

4. If they were unhealthy, what could you have done differently?

_____
_____
_____
_____
_____
_____
_____

5. List healthy things you can do to help you cope with loss.

_____
_____
_____
_____
_____
_____
_____

**Note:** Grief is stressful and tiring it can be hard, but it is **not** an illness. It is **not** an illness! Take time out to mourn, express your feelings as you reflect in your journal ("Grief And Bereavement", n.d).

**Psalm 61: 1-2 (NKJV)**
Hear my cry, O God; Attend to my prayer. From the end of the earth I will cry to You, when my heart is **overwhelmed**; Lead me to the rock that is higher than I.

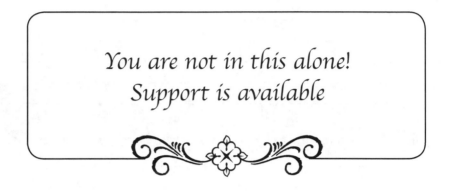

*You are not in this alone!*
*Support is available*

# Journal

# Chapter 3

# The Roller Coaster Ride

*J*ust when I thought, I was on a level plain. My aunt whom was ill with cancer died weeks after the death of my son. What a hit? Boy, her death was a major set-back for me. I woke up around 5:00 a.m., one morning feeling sad, and experiencing what I believe was depression. I had to really force myself out of bed. I had no energy, and I felt somewhat isolated. Friends would call, but I would not return their phone calls until days later. I was not sleeping well, I remember one morning I fell asleep on my sofa and I dreamt I saw my son as a child riding on his bike waving at me through my patio door. Then I saw my brother telling me to let him in.

The inner part of me begin to kick in, and it was as if something was trying to hold me down. I could hear myself saying Jesus, Jesus, Jesus, and all of a sudden my spirit man began to quote this scripture. Yea, though I walk through the valley of the shadow of death, I will fear no evil for thou are with me: thy rod and thy staff comfort me. Because of the biblical teaching I had received I knew it was a familiar spirit in the illusion of my brother. I could hear myself screaming internally. When I awoke, it was as though I had a break through. The same day my friend Deborah came by, and I shared my dream with her. She immediately said the spirit of depression was trying to overtake me. She recognized it right off because she battled with depression. Thank you Jesus, for interceding on my behalf!

Grief is truly a process. I was still feeling the emptiness, but I made a choice to press, I did not want to be stuck. I wanted to grieve in a manner that would not affect my health, and at the same time I wanted to be real with myself and those around me. I needed to be able to acknowledge how I truly felt. I knew that I could do something about my sadness because I had God. I made a choice to reflect on the good times I had with my son. Those reflections made me smile and cry! I was tired of pretending, wearing my mask of normalcy. You know the one we wear…when we don't won't others to see our pain (that fake happiness). I was not going to push, force, nor fool myself and keep pretending as though I was okay. I decided that I was just going to let my natural emotions move me forward. Maintaining my sanity depends upon how I choose to heal. I am glad I am not crazy. All of this is just part of the process, what a relief!

**Note:**

**Depression** *is not grieving.* Grieving the loss of a loved one may include some or all of the symptoms of depression. However, it is important to remember that these feelings of sadness, physical and emotional fatigue are often a normal part of the grieving process. It is possible that an extremely long period of grieving may develop into an episode of depression, but that is a fairly rare experience (Evans, and Radunovich, n.d).

Everyone who has suffered a loss has one thing in common, their Life Changed. Nothing feels the same, and this is what makes us feel, as if, we are going crazy.

1. Are you having signs of depression, if so what are they?

_____
_____
_____
_____
_____
_____
_____

2. What are you doing to help cope with depression?

   _____
   _____
   _____
   _____
   _____
   _____
   _____

3. List activities or projects that you can do to help you cope.

   _____
   _____
   _____
   _____
   _____
   _____
   _____

4. List your favorite songs, movies, and books.

   _____
   _____
   _____
   _____
   _____
   _____
   _____

5. Have you taken any time out to reflect? How do you feel?

   _____
   _____
   _____
   _____
   _____
   _____

**Romans 8: 26-27 (NIV)**
In the same way, the Spirit helps us in our weakness. We do not know what we ought to pray for, but the Spirit himself **intercedes** for us through wordless groans. 27 And he who searches our hearts knows the mind of the Spirit, because the Spirit intercedes for God's people in accordance with the will of God.

My counselor gave the group a paper that said I have a right. It was the "The Mourner's Bill of Rights" by Alan D. Wolfelt, Ph.D. I was happy to know I had a right to feel the way I did. I have included a copy of "The Mourner's Bill of Rights" from the Center For Loss & Life Transition (www.centerforloss.com) on the next page. This will surely help you!

# The Mourner's Bill of Rights
## by Alan D. Wolfelt, Ph.D.

Though you should reach out to others as you do the work of mourning, you should not feel obligated to accept the unhelpful responses you may receive from some people. You are the one who is grieving, and as such, you have certain "rights" no one should try to take away from you.

The following list is intended both to empower you to heal and to decide how others can and cannot help. This is not to discourage you from reaching out to others for help, but rather to assist you in distinguishing useful responses from hurtful ones.

1.  **You have the right to experience your own unique grief.**
    No one else will grieve in exactly the same way you do. So, when you turn to others for help, don't allow them to tell what you should or should not be feeling.

2.  **You have the right to talk about your grief.**
    Talking about your grief will help you heal. Seek out others who will allow you to talk as much as you want, as often as you want, about your grief. If at times you don't feel like talking, you also have the right to be silent.

3.  **You have the right to feel a multitude of emotions.**
    Confusion, disorientation, fear, guilt and relief are just a few of the emotions you might feel as part of your grief journey. Others may try to tell you that feeling angry, for example, is wrong. Don't take these judgmental responses to heart. Instead, find listeners who will accept your feelings without condition.

4.  **You have the right to be tolerant of your physical and emotional limits.**
    Your feelings of loss and sadness will probably leave you feeling fatigued. Respect what your body and mind are telling you. Get

daily rest. Eat balanced meals. And don't allow others to push you into doing things you don't feel ready to do.

5. **You have the right to experience "griefbursts."**
   Sometimes, out of nowhere, a powerful surge of grief may overcome you. This can be frightening, but is normal and natural. Find someone who understands and will let you talk it out.

6. **You have the right to make use of ritual.**
   The funeral ritual does more than acknowledge the death of someone loved. It helps provide you with the support of caring people. More importantly, the funeral is a way for you to mourn. If others tell you the funeral or other healing rituals such as these are silly or unnecessary, don't listen.

7. **You have the right to embrace your spirituality.**
   If faith is a part of your life, express it in ways that seem appropriate to you. Allow yourself to be around people who understand and support your religious beliefs. If you feel angry at God, find someone to talk with who won't be critical of your feelings of hurt and abandonment.

8. **You have the right to search for meaning.**
   You may find yourself asking, "Why did he or she die? Why this way? Why now?" Some of your questions may have answers, but some may not. And watch out for the clichéd responses some people may give you. Comments like, "It was God's will" or "Think of what you have to be thankful for" are not helpful and you do not have to accept them.

9. **You have the right to treasure your memories.**
   Memories are one of the best legacies that exist after the death of someone loved. You will always remember. Instead of ignoring your memories, find others with whom you can share them.

10. **You have the right to move toward your grief and heal.**
    Reconciling your grief will not happen quickly. Remember, grief is a process, not an event. Be patient and tolerant with yourself and avoid people who are impatient and intolerant with you. Neither you nor those around you must forget that the death of someone loved changes your life forever.

# Journal

# Chapter 4

# Nobody Understands How I Feel

*I* was still getting staggered calls with clichés months later. I started reflecting and thinking to myself; you did and said the same thing out of routine when someone else lost a loved one. I begin to say, Oh 'God, help me so I can help others. When other people who lost a child told me they knew how I felt. I would just stare and, unconsciously I would tune them out. In my mind, I was saying you don't have a clue how I feel. You may have lost a child but you have other children and grandchildren. How could you know I feel? Someone still calls you mama. I hated I felt that way because I didn't want to minimize their pain, their grief, their loss, but that was how I was feeling. I would in turn respond with a cliché, and say pray for me. I was angry, and I begin to say nobody understands how I feel.

I later realized if I do not tell people how I honestly feel they will never know. So, now I share my true thoughts with those who say they know how I feel because they too, lost a child. I would say, you may have lost a child, but this was my only biological child who had no kids. I cannot have any more children; therefore the future generation from my son is gone. I have nothing it all died with my son. There will usually be silence then a response of now, I understand. No, I do not know how you feel or what you are going through. It was important to be honest, because pretending it didn't bother me when people told me they understand my pain, only made me angrier. I know they were only trying to be supportive and share momentarily in my grief. Now, they understand how to be supportive without adding to the pain. I realized being honest about my feeling actually helps in my healing.

I was having a hard time one particular morning, so I called my husband and asked him to pray for me, and he did. That morning, I cried out to the Lord. I said God Help Me! I suddenly stop crying and went to my computer. I opened my email, and I saw the word Awesome in the subject line so, I opened it.

This is what it said:

Hi Sis. Williams,

The awesome power of God is beyond measure. Just think about His abilities to do anything. Awesome!

Just a few words to say that I have been praying for you, that God will continue to keep you (Women on The Front Line). **Isaiah 26:3** let us know that God will keep us in perfect peace as we trust and keep our eyes on Him. Then as we trust Him, the peace of God that surpasses understanding shall keep our hearts and minds through Christ Jesus. (Philippians 4:7) (Awesome!) It is the spoken word of God and my personal testimony that allows me to say these words. God is everything you need for any situation faced in life.

My life scripture is Habakkuk 3:19 (AMP) and I want you to daily mediate on it. It states, *"The Lord God is my Strength, my personal bravery, and my invincible army; He makes my feet like hinds' feet and will make me to walk [not to stand still in terror, but to walk] and make [spiritual] progress upon my high places [of 'trouble, suffering, or responsibility]!"*

No matter what you face in life, you can make it through because of the faithful God we serve. God will never leave you, nor forsake you (Joshua 1:5). That's powerful because with God's abilities we can make it through anything. Do know we love you and are continuing to pray for you and your family. Keep up the good work and may God send you His favor.

God Bless!
Minister Rose Howard

After reading this email I got up from my chair, took a step back and looked around. I looked back at the computer to view the time the email was sent, the time said 11:33 a.m. I begin saying I am going to be okay! Rose made it through I am going to be okay, because if anyone actually knows how I feel she does. Rose and her son Joseph were in an accident in which an eighteen wheeler truck veered over on the shoulder of the highway where she was parked. The truck struck their vehicle and her son was killed. I begin to cry in awe of God! I kept saying, if anyone knows how I feel she does! I am going to be okay. I begin to praise and worship God for loving me and hearing my cry. I thank God for showing Himself quicker than quick.

I thank God for the servant he had in place for me and that she obeyed his commandment without delay. She did all of this while at school teaching her kids. I heard and I really appreciated all of the concerns and words of encouragement everyone shared with me. It was when I received that email that it registered, I was going to be okay. Rose could identify with how I was feeling, even though our grief was different, she could really identify, and God had given me something tangible to see. Glory to God! I shared all of this with my class on the same night, and even the counselor was in awe. Today was a good day!

**Note: God will send you what you need just at your breaking point!**

1. Who or what can you identify with concerning your loss? Did it make a difference?

**Note:** Remember loss is loss and grief is grief. Another person ('s) loss does not lessen your loss. It is a personal grief that the person must go through.

**Psalm 138: 1-3 (NKJV)**
I will praise You with my whole heart; before the gods I will sing praises to You. I will worship toward Your holy temple, And praise Your name For Your loving kindness and Your truth; For You have magnified Your word above all Your name. ³ In the day when I cried out, You answered me, *And* made me bold *with* strength in my soul.

God will answer you!

# Chapter 5

# Focusing Through the Tears

My support class had ended, I continued to cry at unpredictable times. I knew I was getting stronger day by day. Crying helped me to heal, and it helped me to release tension that was built up. I am in an ongoing state of releasing my inner emotions, because I want to continue to mourn in a healthy way. I have good days and bad days; I just take one day at a time. I am at a place where I can now see straight. All of my emotions had clouded my vision, and I was just going through the motions.

I begin to weep with gratitude in my heart for all the help and support I had. I could not see, because of all of the pain. I am at a point where I can actually say the pain does not out weight my worship! Let me stop here to share this with you. The key to healing is through our ultimate healer Jesus Christ! He wants to heal you and make you whole in every area of your life. If you are reading this book and you have not accepted Christ as your personal Savior. Why don't you accept Jesus today? You can pray this right now! Lord, I am a sinner forgive me. Jesus I want you to be Lord over my life.

The bible says, if you confess with your mouth the Lord Jesus, and believe in your heart that God hath raised him from the dead, thou shalt be saved (Romans10:9). If you prayed this prayer, welcome to the kingdom of God. Yes! It is just that easy for with the heart man believeth unto righteousness, and with the mouth confession is made unto salvation (Romans 10:10). I encourage you to get into a Bible teaching church for spiritual growth.

1.  Can you see pass the pain (if you cannot answer this question as of yet, remember it is a process and one day you will be able to)?

    _____

    _____

    _____

    _____

    _____

    _____

    _____

    _____

**Note:** When it seems as if you are drowning in your tears, put your focus on Jesus. He will lift you up when you feel like you have no strength left. Just keep wiping your tears and keep focusing on healing healthy.

**2 Corinthians 4:16-17 (NIV)**
*Therefore we do not lose heart. Though outwardly we are wasting away, yet inwardly we are being renewed day by day. For our light and momentary troubles are achieving for us an eternal glory that far outweighs them all.*

*It's okay to cry!*

# Journal

# Chapter 6

# Trying to Work Through It

Months later, I kept saying I am getting better; yet, I was still saying this is crazy! I kept moving; I keep helping others; I kept encouraging and motivating others. I learned to smile on the outside while crying on the inside. I'm dealing with the deaths of my son and aunt and now I have to deal with depleted resources.

You see during the same time period, WEW, Inc. (a non-profit ministry that I founded) had a ministry office, and the day came when I had to close it! I wrote the owner a letter asking for more time to pay him. I told him my son had recently died, and I just did not the money to pay the rent.

The lease was up at the end of the year, I asked him to give me several months and I promised to pay him in full. The ministry resources were exhausted, and I was using my household money for the ministry, and my husband was okay with that. The time came, and I had to count the cost! I had to close the office, and I was hurt and embarrassed, but this was necessary. I moved everything out of the office without any assistance. I would even go to the office on Sunday's to move things out because I did not want anyone to ask me any questions. It took me three months to move.

I kept telling myself a good business person knows when to close an office and start again (In spite of the office closing ministry continued). I was trying to work through everything. I kept my promise and paid the landlord in full. I knew that was God's favor because he did not have to allow me to stay (God was still working on my behalf). I tried reading my bible only to find myself closing it. I could not read it, and I could not pray for anyone else. It took all the strength I had to pray for myself. I was busy trying to understand the things going on in my life. I started many projects, and I was even able to complete some of them. I was having good days and bad days.

I kept going and going! I was happy, sad and depressed! No one really knew it; I was able to mask it well. When I was feeling depressed, I knew to get up and do something. Staying busy helped me focus on other things. I was in a place where no one could help me but God! I would just say Lord, keep me in my right mind. I was getting stronger or so I thought. I was busy working in corporate America, busy at church, busy with ministry. I was a busy bee. I was busy trying to live my new life. It was hard, but I did it! At least that was the perception I gave. I was too busy trying to stay busy! I was trying to avoid dealing with my internal feelings. I was trying to live up to other people's perception that I should be okay by now! I did not want to feel the pain again.

For one year, I slept on my sofa, and I went to sleep after 2:45 a.m. In some instance(s), I was awake 24 hours at a time. I was afraid of receiving a phone call around that time. I did not want to be awaken like that again, (I knew this was out of my control). In all of my busyness, God kept me and gave me favor. I was able to minister to others in the midst of my pain. (Little did I know), I was getting stronger; I just didn't know it. **Shall I say, Believe it!**

1.  How are you doing a now?

   _____
   _____
   _____
   _____
   _____
   _____
   _____
   _____

2.  Are you dealing with your internal feelings? How do you address them?

_____

_____

_____

_____

_____

_____

_____

_____

3.  Are you able to help others even in your pain?

_____

_____

_____

_____

_____

_____

_____

_____

*You will make it!*

# Chapter 7

# Mental Shutdown

Years later, I was trying to function the way I had before and I felt it was working to some degree. However, there was one thing I could not do, it would take my breath away every time I tried. I could not go to the grave site to put flowers on my son's grave. I would send my husband each time, because it was a constant reminder that my son was dead and he was never coming back.

I was busy going, and one day I said I can't do this anymore! I had given all that I had out; I was completely empty. That night I had a dream, and the Lord told me to stop everything (ministry, etc.). He said that our name and the integrity of the ministry mean something. We could not do ministry out of habit. That morning I sent the WEW, Inc. team a letter informing them that we will stop until God says start again. I told them God wants this ministry pure. We had always operated by faith; now we are operating and doing things out of habit. Some people ask how could you stop in the midst of a thriving ministry. Some simply stated the work the ministry provides to the community would be greatly missed. I said I was doing what God said, and He said stop!

God knew what I needed; He allowed me to rest because I was mentally drained. It was then I realized I had not honestly confronted the loss of my son. I had mentally blocked it, and now it was time to deal with it. I cried out Lord, help me to live honestly in my new life. I do not understand, help me to love again! Help me to live! God was growing me in many ways; I just did not know it. I needed to do something for myself. I knew I wanted to grieve healthy because *This is Crazy.*

**Note:** If you do not deal with grief it will deal with you. It will find its way out when you least expect it.

1.  Have you experienced a meltdown? What did you do?

    _____
    _____
    _____
    _____
    _____
    _____
    _____
    _____

2.  How are you doing?

    _____
    _____
    _____
    _____
    _____
    _____
    _____
    _____

3.  Do you have a support base?

    _____
    _____
    _____
    _____
    _____
    _____
    _____

4. Are you wearing a mask?

_____

_____

_____

_____

_____

_____

_____

_____

# Chapter 8

# Finding Self

One day my sister Lisa, called me and told me God said go back to school. I did not question her; I said okay and the next week I enrolled in a university. I had a lot of work experience and some college hours, but no college degree. I always wanted to go back to school, but I would always make excuses, now I realized it was time for me to get my degree. It was time for me to do something for myself! God knew what He was doing.

I have always been a go getter. Whatever I put my mind to do, I would achieve it. Going back to school was very challenging. It took a lot of sacrifice and discipline. Sometimes it got overwhelming, and I wanted to quit. I was working and going to school at the same time. When I looked at my situation, and I realized I was closer to the end than the beginning, and I kept pushing on. Friends told me; I did not have time for them anymore. They did not understand, but I needed to find myself, and I was okay with them feeling that way.

I would let them know I was still their friend; however I needed this time. They loved me thru it, even though we were apart, they were there for me. My time was precious, and it was limited to home, work, church, and school. I had to stay focused on me, in spite of how others may have felt or what they thought. I graduated with an Associate's degree in Business Administration, and later a Bachelor's degree in Human Resources. I give God all the Glory! My future goal is to pursue a Master's degree. It's okay to find yourself, I did it and so can you.

1. What are you doing for yourself?

   _____

   _____

   _____

   _____

   _____

   _____

   _____

   _____

2. Have you been truly honest with yourself?

   _____

   _____

   _____

   _____

   _____

   _____

   _____

*Find the new you!*

# Chapter 9

# God I Want To Live

Six years later, I can honestly say that I am stronger now. I had what I needed all along, my inner strength. I just had to be honest with myself and to trust God. It has been an uphill battle, but I made it. Life is challenging, but worth living. Death has taught me; you do not know how a person feels until it hits your front door. I still have my moments, and this is to be expected, but I decided I wanted to live. I woke up one morning, saying God I want to live (not just exist). I want to be whole in every area of my life. I want to live!

Here is the awesomeness of God, my husband Darryl has an ongoing battle with Parkinson's disease for nine years now. He said this to me "I might have Parkinson, but it does not have to have me, and I want to live"! Now, I understand that statement. I had to make a decision to live! Every day I am working on me. When life gets overwhelming, I reflect on a comment my son told me when he was about 13 years of age "Momma don't sweat that" everything is going to be okay.

My heart is full of gratitude because I can finally say, and mean it, that everything is okay. I do not focus on the loss, but I celebrate the life. I now know, how to live in my new life. I still struggle at times especially when it comes to birthdays and holidays. I smile, as I remember that this struggle is a normal part of moving forward.

I pray this book helps you move forward in life. You have a right to feel the way that you do. You just don't have the right to stay there.

Just know support is available, but you have to want it. I made it and you can too!

Where are you now?

_____

_____

_____

_____

_____

_____

_____

_____

_____

_____

## How has this book helped you?

_____

_____

_____

_____

_____

_____

_____

_____

_____

_____

_____

_____

_____

_____

_____

*Cynthia Williams*

_____

_____

_____

_____

_____

_____

_____

_____

_____

_____

_____

_____

_____

_____

_____

_____

_____

_____

_____

_____

_____

_____

_____

_____

_____

_____

_____

Let us know: www.wewinc.org

# Summary

*I*f you look at me now, you would not think I have gone through anything. The truth is I was in a whirlwind. I was in a place where the only thing I could say was this is crazy! It has taken me seven years to complete my story. Why so long? Partly, because I had mentally blocked my loss. I wanted to be completely honest about the things I was going through. I wanted to say, I am whole and mean it! In this journey I learned a lot about myself. Even during my turmoil and grief, I had what I needed, I just did not know it. God was there all along, He kept me sane in the midst of my insanity. I was in a place where no one could help me but God, and He did.

He orchestrated every phase of my journey. He sent every person and every word that was needed at the right time. This storm could have done one of the two things. It could have broken me to the point I had no will to live or it would drive me to live. In all of it, I had to make a choice. In all of my pain, I had to choose to live. I give God all the Glory for what He has done. When it did not feel like God was there. He was there all the time. I cannot explain how I feel, but I am smiling from the inside out. I leave this with you be honest with how you feel.

Remember being in denial or mentally blocking your loss will only prolong the healing process. Seek to understand, know that you have a right to feel the way that you do. You just do not have a right to stay there. Take the time to find yourself. Please know that it will be scary in your new life. In your shattered world, you will be able to pick up the pieces. God is the only one who can completely heal you, whether you believe this or not. Know that God has purpose for your life, just trust him! It is time to live!

# Scripture Meditation

**Psalm 34:18(NKJV),** "The Lord is near to those who have a broken heart, and saves such as have a contrite spirit."

**Proverbs 3:5-6 (NKJV),** "Trust in the LORD with all your heart, and lean not on your own understanding; in all your ways acknowledge Him, and He shall direct your paths."

**Matthew 5:8, NKJV,** "Blessed are the pure in heart, for they shall see God."

**Romans 10:9-10, NKJV.** "That if you confess with your mouth the Lord Jesus and believe in your heart that God has raised Him from the dead, you will be saved. For with the heart one believes unto righteousness, and with the mouth confession is made unto salvation.

**Ezekiel 36:26**, NKJV. "I will give you a new heart and put a new spirit within you; I will take the heart of stone out of your flesh and give you a heart of flesh."

**Psalm 37:4-**5, NKJV. "Delight yourself also in the LORD, and He shall give you the desires of your heart. Commit your way to the LORD, trust also in Him, and He shall bring it to pass."

**Proverbs 4:23 NIV**, "Above all else, guard your heart, for it is the wellspring of life."

**2 Tim 1:7 (NKJV),** For God has not given us a spirit of fear, but of power and of love and of a sound mind.

**John 14:27 (NKJV),** Peace I leave with you, My peace I give to you; not as the world gives do I give to you. Let not your heart be troubled, neither let it be afraid.

**Deut 31:8 (NKJV),** And the LORD, He is the one who goes before you. He will be with you, He will not leave you nor forsake you; do not fear nor be dismayed.

**Matthew 11:28-30 (NKJV),** Come to Me, all you who labor and are heavy laden, and I will give you rest. Take My yoke upon you and learn from Me, for I am gentle and lowly in heart, and you will find rest for your souls. For My yoke is easy and My burden is light."

**1 Corinthians 10:13(NKJV),** - No temptation has overtaken you except such as is common to man; but God is faithful, who will not allow you to be tempted beyond what you are able, but with the temptation will also make the way of escape, that you may be able to bear it.

**Luke 4:18-19 (NKJV),** "The Spirit of the LORD is upon Me, Because He has anointed Me To preach the gospel to the poor; He has sent Me to heal the brokenhearted, To proclaim liberty to the captives And recovery of sight to the blind, To set at liberty those who are oppressed; 19 To proclaim the acceptable year of the LORD

**Matthew 5:4 (NIV)**
Blessed are those who mourn, for they will be comforted.

**Philemon 4:7** And the peace of God, which surpasses all understanding, will guard your hearts and your minds in Christ Jesus.

# Important Things to Remember

1. It is going to take time.
2. Find the new you- your life has changed.
3. We can get so consumed on what we lost, that we forget about what we have.
4. Learn to embrace your new life.
5. Don't push away those who reach out to you, just tell them to allow you time.
6. Do not be offended when family and friends do not respond to your grief in the way you think they should.
7. When you get overwhelmed talk about it. Be honest with how you are feeling.
8. You are not in this alone-You will make it.
9. Support is available- You have to want it.
10. You will smile from the inside out again.
11. Hurting people hurt other people.
12. Do not be ashamed to get professional help if needed.
13. Celebrate your success. It is okay to move forward.
14. Love again
15. Live again.

# References

Grief and Bereavement. (n.d). Retrieved from http://www.palliative.org/newpc/patients/grief_index.html

Garret Evans, Psy.D. and Heidi Liss Radunovich, Ph.D.2,. (n.d). *Signs and Symptoms of Depression1*. Retrieved from http://edis.ifas.ufl.edu/fy100

Wolfelt, Ph.D., A. (2011). *The Mourner's Bill of Rights*. Retrieved from http://www.centerforloss.com/2014/02/mourners-bill-rights/

# Author

Cynthia is a native of Louisiana. She resides in Dallas, Texas. She is the founder and CEO of Women Empowering Women for the Next Generation (WEW, INC.) Ministries. It is a faith base 501 c3 organization that offers self-help, spiritual renewal, and enrichment programs for women.

She is a businesswoman, a licensed Realtor, a minister, teacher, speaker, conference host and one who seeks to make a change in the lives of people by being transparent with her life for the Kingdom of God. She says, if she can change one life, and that person help to change another life and so on. The world is being changed one life at a time.

She is the recipient of the Joyce M. Jones Community Service Award to name a few. She encourages collaboration; she says we can do more together. Cynthia, believes we do not have to do it all, just do our part. She is a member of National Association of Realtors (NAR), Metrotex Association of Realtors, National Association of Professional Women (NAPW), and The Society for Human Resource Management (SHRM).

She is guided by Philippians 4:13, I can do all things through Christ who strengthens me.